INTERNATIONAL INSTITUTE FOR SUCCESSFUL LIVING, INC.

Workbook 1

ENTANGLEMENT
AND
DETANGLEMENT

Companion Workbook For
"From Ashes to Wisdom"

Healing, Recovery, and Restoration to Destiny

Dr. Maxcelle Yvonne Forrester

authorHOUSE

AuthorHouse™
1663 Liberty Drive
Bloomington, IN 47403
www.authorhouse.com
Phone: 833-262-8899

Published by AuthorHouse 06/16/2022

ISBN: 978-1-6655-5958-4 (sc)
ISBN: 978-1-6655-5957-7 (e)

Print information available on the last page.

Contents

Congratulations and Welcome Aboard!

Today, I congratulate you because you have taken the very first step of realizing and acknowledging that it is necessary to move and change your status from this place. You have started the journey searching for something new, different, better, satisfying, and more in line with your dreams, goals, and expectations. You may want more out of life, but only you can determine what more is and how it will benefit you today and tomorrow. This program will enable you to be confident in identifying what is necessary to make life work on your behalf and in your favor. You can expect positive changes to occur within yourself, so there is no need to be afraid. These are of great value, and the benefits are transferable to your children, family members, friends, and strangers alike for eternity.

This program will be a wonderful gift, especially for those who need help fixing their lives. Many people are hurting, and some have tried other programs that did not help, while others don't know where to go. Feel free to purchase the program as gifts for these individuals. You will be sowing seeds for their recovery. What you make happen for others, God will make it happen for you. If you help, you will receive help. If you give, you will also receive. These are laws that operate in our lives as truths and facts.

Remember that one must qualify to participate in the Rise Program.™ We will not waste your time if we cannot help you or if you are not a good match for this program. The admission process will include an interview.

Welcome aboard! Let's get started! We have work to do, things to pursue, lives to be restored, dreams to fulfill, and places to go. These are exciting times of great anticipation in becoming and attaining all possibilities in this life by redirecting our mindsets and our steps.

Participation in the Program is not automatic

Caution:

Feeling suicidal, have suicidal ideations, or have a history of attempted suicide? This program is not for you unless you are receiving professional care, and it is an adjunct to your recovery. Please consult with your medical practitioner before starting or continuing. It is your responsibility to get medical clearance should you choose to proceed. We will assume that you have received such as we do not require any medical information for participation.

Participants must respect the right to privacy and confidentiality in handling information shared within the group setting. We honor each person's right to be heard, disagree, and be treated with courtesy and respect. Foul language, hateful, demeaning, or insulting words are grounds for dismissal.

It is not a program for those who know it all, who are unteachable, unwilling to try, or want to focus on academia to gain knowledge. It is for those willing to learn, work, adapt to instructions, and are ready for a change.

Goals of the Rise Program™

This section aims to overview goals to help you identify what you can hope to achieve in this program. They will allow you to:

- Move you out of a dysfunctional state to the right and purposeful intentions you are to fulfill.

- Bring additional value, skills, and significance to your growth and development as a whole person instead of remaining a fractured being.

- Identify your lifestyle issues that may be hindering your happiness and overall progress in life.

- Recognize your present setbacks' potential root cause and intervene to prevent your life from going around in circles. These can be circles of pain, suffering, disappointment, despair, failure, etc.

- Learn additional skills to reduce and eliminate stress in life by utilizing insight, knowledge, wisdom, and the revelation of truth.

- Identify character flaws and habits that need to be modified or changed permanently.

- Develop confidence in your ability to govern your life for a better outcome through strategic decision-making.

- Identify destructive thoughts, habits, and behavior patterns that presently do not allow you to make proper decisions.

- Introduce you to the timeless precepts, principles, instructions, and laws that govern successful living by the Creator's will.

- Establish a foundation that contributes to emotional stability and inner peace within and around you.

- Integrate relevant biblical principles and precepts in understanding the effects of sowing and reaping, actions and reactions, and cause and effect relationships.

- Provide teaching and instructions on healing, health and salvation.

- Connect to online access to group coaching sessions with classmates for additional support, encouragement, and partnering in assignments.

- Discover the hidden and untapped talents and gifts that are within you.

- Recognize the potential greatness that surfaces through difficulties.

- Introduce you to the love of your Creator, who personally knows all about you, who understands you, and wants to help you move beyond your present state of being.

- Develop collaborative team-building relationship skills with others in the course.

- Encourage you to recognize and resist lies, falsehood, deception, and hypocrisy by honoring that which is truth.

- Share the lessons learned through your experiences to avoid some pitfalls in life.

- Become a change agent to others by transforming and upgrading yourself and instituting self-care issues as a priority in your life.

A Call to the Rise Program™

The Rise Program™ calls you to arise from where you are and help you move into your purpose and destiny. We are created to succeed in life, and we are not destined for failure unless this is our choice. The program will help you unlock and unfold the mysteries needed to find, repair, discard, or replace the missing or broken pieces to reassemble your life. It will provide you with many keys necessary to unlock the doors to successful living. These keys are timeless and will never change even when societal norms, values, and morals become more confusing, deceptive, without boundaries, and focus on being self-indulgent. The intended goal is a culture without morality, law, and order at every level of society. The traditional family, God, and love for the country were a hallmark of our culture's status. Today, they are being crushed and deemed non-significant, non-essential, and having no relevant purpose except for obstructing or hindering progress in obtaining total freedom void of all responsibilities. Rejection of the foundation that led to success, understanding, predictability, stability, and maintenance of law and order will always result in self-destruction as an individual, community, nation, or civilization.

You will learn principles and precepts that will never change because they have been tested, tried, and proven to be accurate by the One who fashioned and designed all that defines who you are. Our needs and desires as human beings are more similar than different. The Creator has not changed the design or the pattern He has used for making us since the beginning of time. Every system of operation established centuries ago still works today when applied. As human beings, we have changed our expectations, but God has not changed his standards for how we ought to live on the earth. He is the same yesterday, today, and forever. He cannot change (Malachi 3:6, Hebrews 13:8). We institute changes for our convenience and to satisfy our rebellious nature, without the thought of consulting Him, who is the Creator, Author, and initiator of all life, including ours.

When our automobile needs repair, we look to the designer, manufacturer, or mechanic shop for information to diagnose the root cause of the problem. We also look to the repair manual or our training to identify the source. Likewise, with life's issues, we consult the Creator's teaching and instructional manual to determine the root cause and the cause-and-effect relationships to solve the dilemma. The Bible contains all of the laws for successful living; the teaching, instructions, principles, and even the consequences of not carrying them out. As a result, many of the techniques utilized in this program are not mainstream and do not reflect the broader societal views, values, practices, and norms. Bringing our life into order and in alignment with the intent of the Creator is the first step toward wholeness and success, and it moves us from a state of dysfunction, weakness, failure, and brokenness into the right path. Now, we can walk with confidence and the wisdom to ignore and reject the many pseudo alternatives available within our society.

The unsustainable but faulty belief structures, the unprincipled societal forces, and the immoral value systems we have experimented with have contributed to the many woes we are still experiencing. These are often contributing factors leading to our level of dysfunction, confusion, irresponsible decision making, and the many evil manifestations we now witness at home, in the Marketplace, in our schools, and in our world. The hope is for us to detangle the webs of falsehood and partial truths to see clearly and accurately.

The Rise Program ™ accommodates guidance through coaching in a group where participants can freely share their hearts and minds while respecting confidentiality. Encouragement, support, strength, understanding, and validation can be comforting as realized gains in the process. The fostering of an internet community for students' participation and Facilitator guided coaching will provide direction for learning, growth, and reinforcement to strengthen the inner man as we supply each other's needs.

There will be assignments where we will need to connect. The groups will include both new and seasoned participants. Success will be the willingness to adjust and adapt to the information and incorporate them as lifestyle habits. The Rise Program™ integrates self-assessment strategies, coaching, education, meditation, mentoring, and self-improvement techniques to maximize our benefits. It will help gain emotional healing, build strength, and stay healthy.

Upon conclusion of The Rise Program,™ we should focus on maintaining a balanced and healthy lifestyle in every dimension of our being. We are creatures of habit, and our willingness to change requires us to take risks. It is much easier and less taxing to stay settled in a place where comfort, even when this position may be dysfunctional, paralyzing, faulty, or grossly incompatible with living a successful life. We must continually change along the way to meet our future, which is moving towards us daily. Therefore, it is necessary to learn to embrace change as a good thing because this will allow us to make faster adjustments. The ultimate result will be a changed lifestyle to and for the glory of God. Only He gets the credit, although He works through and with others to deliver benefits on our behalf. He declares His intentions for our comfort and reassurance that we are important to Him. He reminds us daily that He is always available, capable, willing, and able to help us succeed.

Progression through the Program

1. You may read or listen to one chapter in the book of Proverbs daily according to the month's date. So, on the 23rd of the month, you will read Proverbs 23 to stay consistent. You can gain much wisdom from this book. When you finish, you should start over and continue through a second time. Every time you read, you will gain more insight, knowledge, and revelation because the Scriptures will always meet you exactly where you are at that moment in time. This process will also help you to remember them through the process of repetition.

2. Read or listen to the Psalm, starting with the first chapter. As you do, you will begin to see a portrait of yourself, your emotions, and your situation. It will help you understand the spiritual realm and its strategies to strengthen, encourage, and elevate your faith. You will realize that you are not alone and that others have risen triumphantly above their circumstances, and so will you. You may cry, smile, and reflect, but you will laugh again and experience joy and happiness from your internal and external environments.

3. The Book of John will introduce you to the Messiah, His leadership abilities, training curriculum, His love for people, and righteous living.

4. You may download the audio Bible on your phone and follow along as you read. We recommend the Nelson Study Bible (New Kings James Version) as preferred but not required. When multiple senses are at work, there is better retention. However, the best practice is sitting, reading aloud, taking notes, and writing a summary of your thoughts, feelings, and any new revelation that you discover as part of journaling.

5. Scheduling a time using the alarm system on your phone to create reminders. Here, you will be taking the time to take care and invest in yourself.

6. The government of God is the first five books of the Bible, and these you will become familiar with, although this program revolves around all sixty-six books of the Bible.

7. Most chapters in this manual have an exercise at the end that may include some scripture references. These are supportive documentation for the manual.

8. Please develop a plan to pace accordingly by putting yourself on a schedule to complete the program within the allotted timeframe. The length of each chapter varies, some requiring more or less time. The time goes by quickly, and it waits for no one, so be diligent in completing your work on schedule.

IT'S YOUR TIME TO ARISE FROM WHERE YOU ARE

Arise, shine;

For your light has come!

And the glory of the Lord is risen upon you.

For behold, the darkness shall cover the earth,

And deep darkness the people; But the Lord will arise over you,

And His glory will be seen upon you.

The Gentiles shall come to your light,

And kings to the brightness of your rising.

Isaiah 60 (NKJV)

Topic: The Rise Program™

Exercise: GPS in the Forest (A Self-Screening tool)

1. Please complete your initial self-assessment tool.

2. Circle the areas that apply to you.

Today's date _____/_____/_____   Next Review _____/_____/_____

Next Review _____/_____/_____   Next Review _____/_____/_____

Instructions: Please Circle all that applies.

1. How do you describe your life today?

Highly Stressed	Feeling Stuck
Broken	Burdened
Sick	Diseased
Worried	In emotional pain
Fatigued	Despondent
Fed-up	Disgusted
Rejected	Abandoned
Abused	In despair
Sad	Grieving
Defeated	Unjustly treated
Ashamed	Feeling guilty
Disrespected	Empty

Feeling lost	Without hope
Sorrowful	Lonely
Lost	Confused
Neglected	Disappointed

_____   _____

_____   _____

2. Please circle the feeling or concerns influencing your life today?

   -   Don't know who you are anymore (loss of identity)

   -   Don't know what you should have known about life (ignorance)

   -   In the pit and no one to help you out (stagnant)

   -   Experiencing a miserable existence (depressed or oppressed)

   -   Emotional traumas (negative experiences)

   -   Heavy laden with guilt and grief (loss, shame, anger)

   -   Misused and feeling trampled upon (loss of boundaries, victimization)

   -   Living life on a roller coaster ride (emotionally challenged)

   -   Have little to show for your years of labor to date (loss or waste)

   -   Taken for granted and not appreciated (loss of value or significance)

   -   Have difficulty turning off bad memories that are actively churning within your mind (unforgiveness or bitterness)

Others:

_____

_____

_____

_____

What do you hope to achieve in this Program?

1.

2.

3.

4.

5.

How will you know when you have achieved the desired results?

1.

2.

3.

Topic: Who will Benefit From the Rise Program?™

Exercise: The Starting Place

Instructions:

1. Answer the questions below as honestly as you can.

2. This is an individual assignment, but you may partner with another to share the experience.

3. Remember to honor the privacy, respect, and confidentiality pledge.

Questions and exercises:

1. How did you arrive at this messy situation in life?

2. Describe your present state of being (happy, sad, broken, desperate, etc.).

    -   How did you arrive at this place, at this moment, and at this time?

    -   Why did you arrive here, at this place and time?

    -   What decisions led you from the beginning to this place?

    -   Can you reverse the directions to get back to your starting place? Start by writing every step or decision you took to get here, then follow these steps backward to get to your starting position. What have you learned from this exercise?

3. Where do you want to go from here, and in which direction should you turn?

4. What do you have on hand to change the overall trajectory of your life?

5. What else do you need to move from this place?

6. Can you hear the call of destiny? What would be an appropriate response?

7. Are you doubtful or confused about the purpose you are to fulfill in this life?

8. What missed opportunities do you presently regret?

   - What caused you not to seize the opportunity?

   - How do you know when the timing is right and when to move quickly?

9. Is this Program an opportunity for change, growth, and development? How would you know if this is the right Program or timing?

10. What is the main reason for your participation in this Program?

11. What self-help programs have you tried before?

- What benefits did you gain?

- What were the drawbacks?

- Why did they not work for you?

- Did these programs include attention to biblical principles?

12. How much time can you comfortably allow investing in this program?

13. How do you plan to schedule this time to pace yourself?

14. Do you have an accountability partner, a cheerleader, or someone to check your progress?

Suggestions: Use an appointment book or computer-assisted devices to schedule your time with attention to the following area:

- Scriptures reading.

- Chapter Overviews.

- The corresponding title assigns exercises in the book.

- Group Coaching Sessions.

- Grand Rounds.

- Your anticipated time frame for completing the Program is _____ weeks on _____/_____/ 20_____.

Topic: A Call to the Rise Program™

Exercise: Narrow Pathway

Instructions:

1. Make this an individual assignment.

2. Become familiar with the goals of this Program.

Questions and Project:

1. Read the goals and identify the top five that apply to your life situation.

    -

    -

    -

    -

    -

2. Rank them in priority from # 1 to #5, with #1 as the most significant five selected.

    -

    -

    -

    -

    -

3. Explain why you ranked that goal as number one and two.

4. Talk to your Creator: Inquire about the plan He has for you to accomplish. Ask Him about the hopes and desires of your heart. Ask Him for clarity, direction, guidance, and help, knowing that He has all the solutions to your problems and the answers to life's issues. Proverbs 3:5, "In all your ways, acknowledge Him, and He will direct your path." We believe Him to honor the scriptures as His words, covenant, and promises because of His love for us. As we draw close to Him, He will draw near to us. He wants us to take the initiative in demonstrating our faith, acceptance, obedience, and our ability to believe. Talking to Him is an act of this initiative, and you can do this as often as you see fit. There are no limitations.

5. Do a scripture search on the word "Wisdom." You may use your phone, computer, or the concordance at the end of your Bible. What does the Bible teach about the importance of wisdom in managing your life?

6. Select one scripture verse from your "Wisdom" review that is meaningful and commit it to memory.

7. Meditate on Proverbs 3:5 throughout the day for three days, and observe how the scripture begins to shape your thoughts, actions, feelings, and priorities.

    -   You can do this because your brain generates new cells for learning. You are never too old to remember information.

- You may use an index card to write each scripture verse to carry it around in your pocket, purse, or vehicle for easy access.

- Always read the verse aloud until you remember it without aid or assistance.

- The use of an index card or voice recording on your phone is an excellent way to learn while making good use of the time spent in traffic.

SAMPLE OF INDEX CARD MEMORIZATION SYSTEM

Heading: Proverbs 3:5

Line #1.   Trust in the Lord

Line #2.   With all your heart

Line #3.   And lean not on your understanding

Line #4   In all your ways

Line #5.   Acknowledge Him

Line #6.   And He will direct your path.

Line #7.   Proverbs 3:5

Topic: Life is the Reflection in Your Mirror

Exercise: No Regrets

Instructions:

1. Make this a group activity and discussion.

2. Include others of your choosing.

3. Continue journaling.

4. Participate in Group coaching.

5. Share what you have learned.

6. Listen to the Books of Proverbs, Psalm, or John.

7. Participate in Grand Rounds.

Questions and Discussion:

1. Explain the significance of these scriptures to your world.

   - Romans 8:28 (The good, bad, and ugly serve a purpose for our benefit).

   - Philippians 4:11-13 (It's vital to find that place of contentment).

   - 1st Timothy 6:6-12 (Learn to be content and not pursue the vanity of ruins).

- Job 36:11 (God values our obedience and service for prosperity).

- Proverbs 14: 30 (The soundness of our heart gives life to our being, and envy within the heart destroys our bones, causing them to rot).

2. Since birth, everything that happened in your life (good, wrong, minor, or tremendous) played a significant role in your life and is for your good (Romans 8:28).

- Describe how does this statement make you feel?

- From which situations did you not gain knowledge, understanding, or insight?

- How has your past experiences influenced who you are today?

- How different would you be without those experiences?

- How has the negative experiences influenced the core of your foundational; beliefs, practices, and decision-making processes?

3. These are the best of times and the worst of times.

- Explain how this statement applies or does not apply to your present life or state of affairs?

- Would you trade or exchange your pieces of baggage for someone else's? Why or Why not?

4. How would you describe the level of contentment in your life? What creates such?

5. Describe a life without stress?

    - Would this be a satisfying life for you? Why or why not?

    - What constitutes a life devoid of stressful situations, occurrences, and events?

6. Life presents us with daily growth-producing opportunities for change.

    - Do you believe this statement to be true or false? Explain your choice.

    - Explain why do we get stuck in a rut?

7. What could you change to bring about improvement in your life?

In your attitude?

In your mindset?

In your image or perception?

In your habits?

In your relationships?

In your faith?

In your work habits?

In your ability to understand and be understood by others?

In time management?

In money management?

In occupation, career choices, or skills development?

In maintaining or gaining health?

In serving others?

In gratitude and appreciation?

In showing love?

In self-care activities?

In finding peace and satisfaction?

In knowing more about your Creator?

In developing a new hobby?

In leisure, travel, volunteering, entertainment of family and friends?

Topic: Understanding Yourself Through the Eyes of the One Who Made You

Exercise: The Bond

Instructions:

1. Be familiar with the scriptures in the chapter.

2. Identify areas requiring more understanding or exploration.

3. Ask your Creator for wisdom.

4. Continue journaling.

5. Share what you have learned with others.

6. Participate in Group coaching.

7. Continue listening to the Books of Psalm, Proverbs, or John.

Questions:

1. What are the characteristics mentioned about the Creator?

2. Creation exists through God's wisdom. What tangible evidence in the universe supports this?

3. How does knowledge of the Creator promote a closer relationship with Him?

4. Life's decisions do not grant us the position of being neutral, and we must choose one of the two kingdoms. What are some differences between these kingdoms, and how do they influence your choices?

5. What are possible reasons for God creating good and evil? What purpose do they serve in life?

6. What is the Instructional Manual for Life, and what purpose does it serve?

7. What is the purpose for the Creator to instill a conscience within us?

8. How do you recognize your conscience at work in judging your motives, decisions, and sensitivity towards what is right, wrong, trustworthy, fair, equity, and just?

Topic: A Firm and Stable Footing

Exercise: The Hidden Me

Instructions:

1. Be Familiar with the scriptures in this chapter.

2. Participate in the Group coaching sessions.

3. The assignment can include family or friends.

4. Participate in Grand Rounds.

5. Continue journaling.

6. Share what you have learned with others.

7. Continue listening to the Books of Proverbs, Psalm, or John.

Questions:

1. How are you similar to your parents or individuals in the family line?

2. What similar characteristics do you share with the Creator?

3. If there is no Creator, how does one determine their identity apart from physical features?

4. What relevant information did you learn about the Creator?

5. What have you learned about yourself from this chapter?

6. What have you learned about the workings of the enemy?

7. What information surprised you most about who you are in God-Yeshua?

8. What new information or principles could you immediately integrate into practice?

Topic: You Are the Crown Creation

Exercise: For the Beginning to Eternity   #Stop

Instructions:

1. Be familiar with the scriptures in this chapter.

2. Include others.

3. Continue journaling.

4. Participate in Grand Rounds.

5. Participate in Group coaching.

6. Share what you have learned.

7. Listen to the Books of Proverbs, Psalm, or John.

Questions and Discussion:

1. Explain the significance of Jeremiah 29:11 to your life.

2. How would you describe a soul that is dead?

3. What does the Spirit-spirit connection mean, and what is its significance?

4. If Messiah (Jesus Christ) gives us life, then those without Him are dead. Explain 1ˢᵗ John 5:12 and the implications to your life.

5. What thought processes or perspectives have you identified that can help improve your life?

Topic: You are in the Creators Lineage: You are Royalty

Exercise: Prince and Princess

Instructions:

1. Become familiar with the scriptures in this session.

2. Please answer the questions below.

3. You may include others in this exercise for discussion purposes.

4. Provide input in the group coaching session.

5. Continue journaling.

6. Listen to the Books of Psalm, Proverbs, or John.

7. Share what you have learned with others.

8. Participate in Grand Rounds.

Questions:

1. In establishing any type of relationship, what are ten character traits you would consider incompatible with your core beliefs, design, purpose, and destiny in life?

2. We are all born equipped with everything needed to succeed. What would cause someone to fail when God has already installed the template for success?

3. Have you ever experienced success in your life?

  - When?

  - How did it feel?

  - Who helped you?

  - What were the circumstances surrounding your achievement?

  - How did you celebrate victory?

  - What are the chronological steps you took from the beginning to the end?

  - Could you repeat success with the same steps? If not, why not?

  - What kind of success do you hope to achieve in life?

  - What three obstacles, challenges or issues did you encounter?

  - How were they resolved?

- What three character traits allowed you to overcome or succeed?

- What prevents you from fulfilling your dreams today?

4. Pride is an internal and destructive force that always guarantees a fall.

   - How does pride presents itself?

   - Can you identify any prideful tendencies within you?

5. "There is no me without you."

   - What does this statement mean to you?

   - How do others contribute to your daily existence?

   - What roles do your friends play in your life?

   - What are three things that you do consistently to reciprocate in your friendships?

- Write a brief note to three friends expressing your appreciation of the relationship and explain how they contribute to your wellbeing. Pay attention to their responses.

- What did you learn from writing the notes of appreciation?

6. What role does the blood of Jesus play in salvation, redemption, deliverance, healing, and forgiveness of sin or dysfunction?

Topic: None

Exercise: Time and Season

Instruction:

1. This is a two-person assignment.

2. Participate in Grand Rounds.

3. Participate in Group coaching.

4. Share what you have learned with others.

5. Continue journaling.

6. Listen to the Books of Proverbs, Psalm, or John.

Questions:

1. Read Ecclesiastes 3:1-8. What are the 28 different seasons listed?

2. How do you prepare for the seasonal changes in life?

3. "When life changes, you are the one who must change." How does this apply to your life?

4. There is nothing new under the sun "what is, has already been!" How can one find comfort in this statement?

5. How does integrating the Messiah (Jesus Christ) help us gain spiritual alignment with the Father?

6. What behavior, actions, or personality would indicate that one's heart is insensitive or hardened against the Creator?

7. How would you describe your relationship with the Creator? He created you, but does He know you within the boundaries of a relationship?

8. What does the following scripture mean to you? Whoever does not love does not know God because God is love (1ˢᵗ John 4:8).

9. How do you start a conversation with God?

   (Know that it is easy to engage the Lord by inviting Him into your heart and start any conversation with Him as you would with a friend).

Topic: You May Be a god, But You Are Not God

Exercise: One Living God

Instruction:

1. Review the scripture references.

2. This is a two-person assignment.

3. Participate in Grand Rounds.

4. Participate in Group coaching.

5. Continue journaling.

6. Share what you have learned.

7. Listen to the Books of Proverbs, Psalm, or John.

Questions and Answers:

1. What are the five differences between a false versus the true and living God?

2. How do you define justice, and how does it relate to God's justice?

3. Train your children in the way they should go, and when they are old, they will continue to live the same lifestyle (Proverbs 22:6). How should you train them?

4. Are there areas of weakness that may have resulted from inadequate training or preparation for adulthood?

   - What are they?

   - How have they influenced your adult life?

   - What strategies helped you change or minimize their impact?

5. What is the purpose of discipline, and how and when should it occur?

6. What are five areas of responsibilities that parents have towards raising wholesome children?

7. Why is it important to teach the truth in love?

8. Why is spirit and soul development the most critical aspect of the commandments?

Topic: Foundation of Love

Exercise: Season a Calling

Instruction:

1. This is a two-person assignment.

2. Truthfully answer the questions below to the best of your ability.

3. Continue journaling.

4. Participate in Grand Rounds.

5. Participate in Group Coaching.

6. Share what you have learned with others.

Questions, Instructions, and Discussion:

Please Read & Meditate on Ecclesiastes 3:1-8.

1. We thrive and succeed in a structured, loving, and caring environment. How can this be achieved in your life?

2. Can you give love to someone when you do not love yourself?

3. What mindset is needed to love yourself as a priority?

4. Can you determine the times and seasons that influence your life today?

5. In nature, we have four distinctive seasons (spring, summer, fall, and winter) that relate to how life treats us. What are some of the defining characteristics of each season?

6. Are you at the beginning, middle, or exiting the end of your current season?

    -   Can you describe what it feels like and how you are coping?

    -   How should we prepare for the transitions in the seasons?

7. What pleasures or woes are you presently experiencing in this season?

8. Every season has a distinct beginning and an end. Have you ever felt like you have overextended your time in one area where you feel stuck, stagnant, or unproductive? What issues are you facing here?

9. Time waits for no one, but it keeps moving forward on its own accord. Are there any areas or issues you feel you have not solved, resolved, or conquered to your satisfaction? Can you identify what they are?

Section: None

Exercise: I See Me   #stop

Instructions:

(1) Please take the time to review the scriptures in this section.

(2) Connect with another student and interview each other using the questions provided.

(3) Share your interviewing experience during Group coaching.

(4) Participate in Grand Rounds.

(5) Continue journaling.

(6) Listen to audio Bible, the Books of Proverbs, Psalm, or Job.

Questions:

1. Why did you choose this Program?

2. Why are you starting now?

3. What Programs have you tried before to help deal with your issues?

4. What convinced you that this is the right program for you?

5. What are you willing to offer towards your growth, development, or recovery?

6. What are the three immediate issues, problems, concerns, or conflicts you feel comfortable sharing?

7. Are you aware that Judeo-Christian principles are integrated into this program?

8. Are you aware that the guidelines for living are for your benefit? What do you think some of these benefits are?

Session: All of Me and All of You

Exercise: Undue Influence

Instructions:

1. This is a two-person assignment.

2. Participate in Grand Rounds.

3. Participate in Group Coaching.

4. Share what you have learned with others.

5. Continue journaling.

6. Listen to the Books of Proverbs, Psalm, or John.

Questions and Project:

1. Share an experience where you believed you made the right decisions, but the outcomes were not what you expected. How did you feel about this?

2. What did you expect to experience and receive, and what were the actual results?

3. How did the results affect you emotionally, physically, financially, spiritually, socially, or otherwise?

4. Looking back at your experiences, what might you have done differently (even if the outcomes were negative or positive)?

5. Did you seek God's direction in prayer before making those decisions?

6. If not, why not?

7. What lessons did you learn from your experiences to impart to someone else?

8. Did you pray the scriptures that pertain to your situation? (Sometimes we pray amiss (James 4:3). We should pray and remind God of His words and promises in the manner as a lawyer would use the statutes, laws, ordinances to defend his cause and his client in the courts based upon previous judgments or precedence). Write a scripture prayer of your choice.

9. Read Psalm 23. This chapter gives insight into who your God is and what you can expect Him to do in your life.

10. How does Psalm 23 relate to your present state of being, and which verses provide comfort to you and why?

11. Practice writing a scripture prayer based upon Psalm 23:1.

For example, in Psalm 23:1, "The Lord is my Shepherd, I shall not want."

Lord, I thank you because you are my Shepherd. As my Shepherd, you belong to me, and I belong to you, and we honor our covenant relationship with each other. You watch diligently over my soul, my life, family, leaders, and friends. I thank you because you can see above me and 360 degrees around me, and you cover me to make sure I am safe from all harm and danger.

There is never a time when you are not watching over me. I trust you because, as my Shepherd, you protect me, lead me, guide me, care for me, and provide for me. I depend totally upon you for my daily needs, desires, and provision. I know that your love for me will never fail. I honor you, and I thank you for everything you have done on my behalf. I bless you in the name of Yeshua (Jesus). Amen.

12. Now, write your prayer (no more than one page).

Please Note:

As you read the Bible, pay particular attention to verses or sayings you wish to remember and include in future prayers. I have added other sources to the prayer, such as You are my source, and you have promised that the righteous and their seed will never beg for bread because You are merciful (Psalm 37:25-26).

You provide food for the birds of the air, the insects, and the animals because they depend upon you for their daily food and the rains from heaven to bring water into the earth. You promise to supply all my needs according to your riches in glory (Philippians 4:19). Thank you for my employment, making it possible to purchase food and meet my daily needs. Thank you for lunch donated to us today; you know I did not have a dollar in hand.

Father, I pay my tithes and give an offering to express my covenant with you. Thank you for opening the heavens above my family and me that there will never be a lack in our home. God, you said you would rebuke the devour for my sake because of my commitment to obey and plant seeds of righteousness into your kingdom. You promise to multiply my resources on earth for my obedience (Malachi 3:11).

Thank you for your faithfulness to me. I declare that whatever things I ask for when I pray, I will receive it according to Mark 11:24. So I ask for your favor, grace, blessings, increasing supplies, and provisions in the name of Yeshua, and I also seal this prayer with His Spirit. I thank you for answered prayer— Amen (So let it be!).

Basic Understanding of the Kingdom

Exercise: From Life to Death to Life PART 1

Instructions:

1. Review the diagram, which illustrates "The Cycle from Life to Death to Life."

2. Participate in Grand Rounds.

3. This is a joint project with no more than three persons of choice.

4. Participate in the Group coaching session.

5. Continue journaling.

6. Share what you have learned.

7. Listen to the Books of Proverbs, Psalm, or John.

Questions and Project:

1. Define obedience.

2. Define disobedience.

3. Explain the benefits of adopting your lifestyle to the principles of the kingdom of God.

4. Where in the Bible can you find three principles of God? Write the scripture and the address (Book, chapter, and verse).

5. Define salvation, and what are the benefits to the individual?

6. What is the law of sin and death, and how does it impact our lives?

7. What is eternal life, and why should this be important to us?

8. How do you define spiritual death, and what significance does this play in our lives?

9. What is the difference between physical death and spiritual death?

10. What would one experience in a life separated from the love of God?

11. What conditions, issues, or circumstances would produce soul injury or death to the soul?

12. What is the difference between health and healing? Who is responsible for each?

13. What is the definition of eternal life and eternal death? How do they differ?

Exercise: From Life to Death Part 2

14. Define redemption.

15. Define restoration.

16. Define deliverance.

17. Define justification.

18. How do the scriptures bring about restoration, deliverance, justification, and redemption?

19. The Torah is the first five books of the Bible and all 66 books. What are the first five?

20. Yeshua's role in restoring humanity to its original status as is the Garden of Eden. How would you describe the setting at the beginning before the fall of Adam?

21. How does this diagram, "The cycle of life to death to life," reveal God's love for humanity?

22. What is the role and significance of repentance and confession in our lives?

23. What are some significant differences between the kingdom of life and the kingdom of darkness?

24. If you were the Creator of humanity, how would you deal with those who reject the principles you established for them to follow?

25. What can you theorize about the nature and character of our Creator?

26. What are the impacts of obedience and disobedience on the quality of life?

Topic: How Well Do You Know Yourself?

Exercise: Created for Wholeness

Instructions:

1. Read the scriptures associated with this section.

2. Answer the questions as honestly as you can.

3. Consider this as a two-person project.

4. Participate in Grand Rounds and participate in Group coaching.

5. Continue journaling.

6. Listen to the Books of Proverbs, Psalm, or John.

Questions:

1. What positive adjectives would you use to describe yourself?

2. What new adjectives would you use to describe the new you in Yeshua?

3. What adjectives did your parents or guardians use to describe you?

4. How do your siblings or relatives describe you? What names or adjectives do they use when referring to you?

5. What would your teachers write about you in their recommendation letter to the institution of higher learning?

6. What qualities do your employer like most about you as a worker? And what do they like least about you?

7. What characteristics do you value in your friends and associates?

8. What activities do you enjoy sharing with your friends?

9. What characteristics do you admire most about your mother (or surrogate) during your childhood?

10. What characteristics do you admire most about your Father (or the male figures) during your childhood?

11. What characteristics do you see within yourself that you inherited or learned from your parents? Which ones do you embrace fully, and which ones would you choose to modify or eliminate, and explain why?

12. By what process do you unlearn beliefs, habits, and behaviors?

13. When you look in the mirror, tell us about the person looking back at you?

- What do you love most about that person?

- How do you hope to see this person five years from today?

- How would you celebrate this person today?

- How would you celebrate this person in five years?

- Who is this person's best cheerleader, and why?

Repeat this prayer if you desire to make changes in your life today.

Father in Heaven, the God of Abraham, Isaac, and Israel, I open my spirit, heart, mind, thoughts, and soul to you from this day forward. I desire the following changes _____ in my life. I invite you to come into my heart to enjoy the favor, blessings, inheritance, and promises due to me according to your written words.

I realize that the plan you have for me is good, and it is a plan to prosper me and help me become more like you. I believe that Jesus lived and died for the sole purpose of restoring my life for a right relationship with my Creator.

I repent for these known and intentional offenses (sins) against you. List offenses_____. Please forgive me of all unknown and unintentional transgressions (sins). I accept Yeshua as Lord of my life. He forgives and removes these wrongdoings from my life, including the penalty for succumbing to the temptations from the enemy. Thank you for forgiving me and cleansing me of all unrighteousness.

All that I am and ever hope to become, I give to You so that I will inherit and have access to everything that is already mine. I am claiming them in the name of Yeshua. Please help me walk in the path of righteousness, for your name's sake.

Thank you for pursuing after me, guiding, keeping, and adopting me into your kingdom of life, light, and goodness. Help me find rest in You, as I cease from my labor, and partner with you in this life and forever (Jeremiah 1:4-5, Jeremiah 29: 11-14a). Amen.

Topic: Hurting People Hurt People

Exercise: Spare the Pain

Instructions:

1. This is a two-person assignment.

2. Participate in Grand Rounds.

3. Participate in Group coaching.

4. Share what you have learned with others.

5. Continue journaling.

6. Listen to Books of Proverbs, Psalm, or John.

Questions:

1. Why do hurting people tend to hurt others?

2. What are the effects of injuring others by words or deeds?

3. Are the perpetrators aware that whatever they do to others will be done to them also? Would knowing make a difference in how they treat innocent people?

4. Our feelings often determine what we say and do. How do the scriptures frame our emotions to do good to ourselves and others?

5. What role does prayer play in protecting and dealing with our enemies?

6. How would a foolish person approach life's challenges, and what are the anticipated outcomes?

7. How would a wise person approach the challenges of life, and what are the anticipated outcomes?

8. What role does the Spirit of God play in helping our daily walk?

9. When and how should one confront the expressions of anger?

Topic: Manifestations of the Orphan's Spirit

Exercise: Take on the Spirit of Messiah

Instructions:

1. A two-person assignment.

2. Participate in Grand Rounds.

3. Participate in Group coaching.

4. Share what you have learned.

5. Continue journaling.

6. Listen to the audio Books on Proverbs, Psalm, or John.

Questions:

1. What are six manifestations of the orphan's spirit?

2. How do we develop a trusting relationship with those who don't trust us?

3. How would these individuals relate to God as Father when they have not known fathering?

4. How do we build our identity to reflect the Spirit of Christ?

5. How do we minister healing to the injured and traumatized soul?

6. How do we introduce the subject of serving others to selfish-driven individuals?

7. People are willing to change when they identify the benefits of doing so. What obstacles prevent one from seeing the benefit derived from a changed life?

8. Write a scripture prayer for someone with an orphan's heart.

9. What would be the role of an accountability partner in helping this broken soul?

10. What role does acceptance, confession, repentance, truth, and forgiveness play in the lives of an orphan's heart?

Topic: Secrets Influence Our Behavior Patterns

Exercise: Be Made Whole

Instructions:

1. Make this a two-person assignment.

2. Participate in Grand Rounds.

3. Participate in Group coaching.

4. Share what you have learned with others.

5. Continue journaling.

6. Listen to the Books of Proverbs, Psalm, or John.

Project:

1. Ask God to forgive you for known or unknown violations. Make a list of known infractions and present the list to Him. He is faithful and just to forgive us of ALL unrighteousness.

2. Healing starts from the SPIRIT---- to the SOUL------to the BODY. What would indicate that you are healed or in the process of being healed?

3. Read the passage below and answer the questions.

Forgiveness is the most important in cleansing and healing the damaged soul. We cannot be fully healed until we experience richness in our souls. Our spirits, emotions, and bodies will experience health when our souls align with God's plan.

The damaged soul affects and brings forth sickness, disease, and poverty within our bodies and our lives. When we heal the soul, we can heal and change the whole person. The soul belongs to God, where He resides, and the commandments work at the soul level. We learn to adapt to God and others by showing flexibility and establishing priorities.

The soul consists of our will (choices & decisions), memory, emotions, motivation, imagination, and intellect. The soul is the seat of our emotions.

Learn to follow instructions. Every act of faith requires the ability to believe and follow instructions, and faith without works is dead faith, and it has no significant value. We must love others on the same level to which we love ourselves. Unfortunately, many people do not like or love themselves and thus do not have the capacity or the tolerance to give or receive love.

4. How does one strengthen the Spirit to spirit bonding with Messiah to ensure healing?

5. What are the components that make up the soul?

6. What role does the soul play in our lives?

7. How do we receive healing in our souls?

8. How do we receive healing in our bodies?

9. How do secrets become a destructive force in our lives?

10. What strategies relieve the burdens of a secretive lifestyle?

Topic: The Struggle Within

Exercise: Caterpillar

Instructions:

1. Answer the questions as truthfully as you can.

2. This is a two-person assignment.

3. Please be prepared to share at the Group coaching session.

4. Participate in Grand Round.

5. Share what you have learned with others.

6. Listen to the Books of Proverbs, Psalm, or John.

7. Continue journaling.

Questions:

1. List 3 characteristics or traits that automatically stir a feeling of hate. Remember that we distinguish between hating the individual and hating the sin. God loves sinners (John 3:16). Yet, He hates the very resemblance of a sinful nature, act, or characteristics.

2. What are three things that you see in others that could cause you to wave a wand and make them disappear instantly?

3. If the things I hate in others are a true reflection of that which is within me, then who am I, and what is within me that I need to evaluate and change?

4. Who do you look to for affirmation regularly, and why?

5. What similarities and differences did you observe between you and your parents/guardians when you were a child that is still evident in your life today that you want to modify?

6. What three characteristics or habits in your life that you identify as troublesome for you?

7. What have you done to alter these characteristics and habits that are obstacles in your life?

8. Were you successful in making the alterations that you desired? If not, why not?

9. The "me I see within is me, I will become." What are your thoughts about this statement?

   - What reflection do you see when you look in the mirror that makes you smile with appreciation?

   - What do you like best about this person?

10. "The things that I admire and celebrate in others are also within me." Why is this true?

11. "The things that I dislike or criticize in others are also within me." Why is this true?

12. "I am the mirror through which you see yourself." Why is this true?

13. "To the pure, all things are pure. But to those who are defiled and unbelieving, nothing is pure; but even their mind and conscience are defiled (Titus 1:15; NKJV). What is your interpretation of this scripture? How does it influence how we see people and how others see us?

14. "What others say about me matters, but what I say about myself and to myself (self-talk) matters most." Why?

   - We do a lot of self-talk. What do you say to encourage yourself in the Lord?

   - What do you tell yourself about yourself that corresponds with God's view?

   - What do you believe about yourself that equips you for future successes?

   - When did you last correct your self-talk to reflect the person God says you are?

15. What behaviors, characteristics, or habits do you wish to add to your profile?

16. If you are given three wishes to improve something about yourself, what would these be?

17. Are you in love with yourself?

18. Would you date yourself above all others, and would you choose to marry the person you are as a mate? Explain your answer.

19. How would you describe your relationship with yourself today?

20. You are always the most significant person in your life. How would you describe the ideal relationship with yourself?

21. The power of recognition and acknowledgment in life is in the following statements below. How would you apply these statements of truth to your present situation, and how could they have influenced the decisions in your past life?

    - "What we fail to recognize we cannot acknowledge, promote, respond to, care for, respect, or admire."

    - "Whatever we do not acknowledge do not get rewarded by attention, love, or elevation."

- "Whatever we do not recognize, acknowledge, or reward will diminish, withdraw from us and eventually exit our lives."

- "Whatever we do not feed will not grow but will starve and then die in our lives."

- "Therefore, whenever we withhold the required nutrients for sustaining life (in a good or bad situation), it will eventually die or exit my life."

- "How will your awareness influence the quality of your decisions in the future?"

Topic: Reflection

Exercise: Hindsight or Foresight Part 1

Instructions:

1. This is a two-person assignment.

2. Participate in Grand Rounds.

3. Participate in Group coaching.

4. Share what you have learned.

5. Continue journaling.

6. Continue listening to the Books of Proverbs, Psalm, or John.

Questions:

1. Reflection or hindsight provides an opportunity to evaluate life's journey thus far. What has been your greatest accomplishment, and explain why?

2. What are the three most significant lessons you have learned?

3. Foresight allows us to use previous information to plan for the future. What are the three things you wish to accomplish in your life, and when and how do you plan to achieve them?

4. What is the difference between gaining information and wisdom?

5. How would you describe the following?

    -   A moral earth?

    -   A moral universe?

    -   A moral center in man (the conscience)?

6. Heaven and earth bear witness to God's words and dispense blessings and curses. Why are they able to function in this capacity?

7. Our walk with God is a fight of faith. With whom do we fight, and what strategies do we use to win the battles?

8. How does the Bible equip us to deal with the challenges of life, warfare, and success?

9. Describe the profile, nature, and characteristics of a person who functions as a God.

10. God created evil and evil inclination within the hearts of men. What is the purpose and benefit of evil?

11. God created life and death. How do these influence how we choose to live our lives?

12. What is the difference between a vessel created for honor and dishonor?

13. Ignorance makes us vulnerable to self-destruction. Is this true or false, and why?

14. What are the anticipated outcomes of obedience and disobedience?

15. What strategies does Satan use to make our lives miserable?

16. How does Satan help fulfill God's will on the earth?

17. The law is holy, and the commandment holy and just and good (Romans 7:12). How does this help to describe God's nature and character?

The Winning Edge

Exercise: Your Call

Instructions:

(1) Review your life thus far and identify when someone spoke into your life for your benefit and encouragement.

(2) Review all the scriptures.

(3) Conduct an interview with someone who you know and will grant permission.

(4) Share your experience during Group Coaching.

Questions:

1. Who was the most influential person during your childhood years and adult life, and why?

2. Who taught you the difference between right and wrong, clean and unclean, righteous and unrighteous, God and Satan, life and death, life on earth, and eternal life?

3. How were you influenced to define success in life?

4. What kind of character does one need to develop to succeed?

5. Who is ultimately responsible for your success or failure in life?

6. "Now unto Him who is able to keep you from stumbling, and to present you faultless before the presence of his glory with exceeding joy (Jude 1:24)," to God our Savior. What is your understanding of this scripture, and how does it apply to your life?

7. What cautions or precautions should you take in walking the straight and narrow road to success?

8. What were the instructions that you still remember today that you consistently implement in your life?

9. Was church attendance, church school, Bible study, or worship services significant in your upbringing? How do these influence your thought life today?

10. Do you presently practice your faith? On a scale of 1-10, with ten as the highest priority, where is your faith now?

11. If you walked away from your faith, what were the triggering events?

12. How are you building your spiritual faith today?

Topic: Come Clean

Exercise: Wash Yourselves   #stop

Instructions:

1. This is a two-person assignment.

2. Continue journaling your progress.

3. Participate in Group coaching.

4. Participate in Grand Rounds.

5. Share what you have learned.

6. Listen to the Books of Proverbs, Psalm, or John.

Questions:

1. What are your thoughts after reading the chapter?

2. Whom have you blamed for failures and disappointments in your life instead of taking responsibility for your thoughts, choices, decisions, and actions?

3. List the progressive process of decline from offenses to murder or suicide?

4. What advice would you give to someone who is easily offended?

5. Explain how the enemy works within us when we refuse to repent for wrongdoings.

6. How do we elevate the God living within each other?

7. Do a scripture search on any three of the following words of interest:

- Repentance

- Forgiveness

- Obedience

- Lawlessness

- Faith

- Healing

- Murder

- Guilt

- Offense

- Love

- Redemption

- Steadfast (steadfastness)

- Meditation

- Faithful (faithfulness)

- Life

8. How has this chapter changed your thoughts and beliefs about forgiveness?

Topic: Like Your Daddy Parts 1 & 2

Exercise: Fruit Falls Close to the Tree

Instructions:

1. Review the scriptures provided in this section.

2. Participate in Group coaching.

3. Share what you have learned.

4. Continue journaling.

5. Participate in Grand Rounds.

6. This is a two-person assignment.

7. Listen to the Books of Proverbs, Psalm, or John.

Questions:

1. What criteria do you utilize to determine if you should engage in a conflict or contentious discussion?

2. What criteria do you utilize in determining if you should continue a conflicting or contentious discussion?

3. How do you determine when to engage in conflict, avoid it, and stop it?

4. What are the five qualities you look for in determining who should be a part of your innermost circle of friends?

5. How do you qualify people to access your mind, heart, life, and all the treasures you possess?

6. How many layers of friendship do you presently have in your life?

7. What boundaries have you established to ensure that a thief does not enter or have access to the personal or secret things you possess within you?

8. What are the five most critical red flags you look for to eliminate or prevent access to your heart?

9. How do you contribute positively to the welfare of others in elevating their status in life?

10. The Ten Commandments that God wrote with His finger are the laws of living. The first five commandments focus on our relationship with Him, and the other five deal with our connection to each other.

   - Write the ten commandments (Exodus 20).

11. Which three Commandments do you desire to learn? Can you locate three scriptures that refer to these commandments?

12. There are 613 principles, precepts, lifestyle habits, and characters from the ten commandments we should develop. It is not humanly possible to keep all of them without the Spirit of God prompting us. Can you remember when you wanted to say or do something, and you didn't, just because of "a gut feeling, an intuition, or something telling you what to do?" What was the circumstance?

13. How does the Spirit of God operate within your life? (1st Kings 19:11-13)

   - How does it speak to you?

   - When do you choose to ignore it?

   - When do you choose to listen to it?

   - Has there been a situation or occasion that you regret not listening to the advice of your conscience?

   - What was the situation or event?

   - What was the outcome, and how were you able to make amends?

- What lessons have you learned from your conscience?

- How will you apply the lessons learned?

14. What other things listed below would you consider in making a decision and explain why?

- Consultation with your Creator (should be your first choice)

- Bible Review

- Research

- Expert advice

- Counselor

- Coaching

- Advice from elderly/wise individuals

-

-

15. What is the Fruit of the Spirit? (Galatians 5:22-23)

- List one fruit that needs to be in your life.

- How will maturity help to make your life better?

- What can you do to grow in this area?

16. What else do you need to move from a place of stagnation?

- Think differently

- change your mindset

- give different sets of instructions to follow your brain

- change your habits by doing something different instead

- select new associations for where you want to grow and go

- change the setting, location, or environment

-

-

17. What behavior patterns do you need to break, destroy, eliminate, or erase in your life to become your best?

  - What new thoughts do you need to believe or think to make the change?

  - Evaluate why and how these patterns developed and what purpose or benefits they serve in your life.

  - Determine what new behaviors need to replace the problematic ones to improve your life?

  - How do you stop doing the former behaviors that created the dysfunctional patterns?

  - How do you replace and institute the new patterns you have chosen above?

(Note: "The acts of doing" matter most. Behavior patterns, including habits, can be replaced, deleted, or broken. Rarely is it instantaneous, but this can be accomplished over three or more weeks of consistent work).

- What is your allotted timeframe for completion?

- Self-control and mind over matter work when you diligently apply the new patterns. What instructions do you need to give your mind?

Note: (Your brain must obey the information or instruction given to your mind, thoughts, or heart. The brain must listen to your voice. You are the master controller of your brain).

Topic: You are what you Say

Exercise: Shut Your Mouth

Instructions:

1. Do this session with a partner of your choice.

2. Memorize one scripture verse that reminds you to think before speaking.

3. Be prepared to participate in Group Coaching.

4. Participate in Grand Rounds.

5. Share what you have learned.

6. Continue journaling.

7. Listen to the Books of Proverbs, Psalm, or John.

Questions:

1. Explain your understanding of life's application to the statements below.

   - "So shall My word be that goes forth from My mouth; it shall not return to me void. But it shall accomplish what I please, and it shall prosper in the things for which I sent it (Isaiah 55:11).

   - If you don't have anything good to say, remain silent.

- Life and death are in the power of the tongue, and they that love it shall eat the fruit thereof.

- The words from your mouth will be the meal that your life must digest.

- Let the words of my mouth and the meditation of my heart be acceptable in thy sight, O Lord, my strength, and my redeemer (Psalm19:14).

- It's not what is said but how one says it that matters most.

- For as a man thinks in his heart, so is he (Psalm 23:7).

- It's not what goes into a man that defiles him, but what comes out (Matthew 15:11).

- Some people are wise when they hold their peace but foolish when they open their mouths (Proverbs 17:28).

- A man who cannot control his mouth or emotions cannot control his life.

- The parents have eaten the sour grapes, and the children's teeth are on edge (Jeremiah 31:29).

- An angry person is experiencing a temporary state of insanity.

- In your anger, do not sin (Ephesians 4:26).

- Why is it essential not to let the sun go down on your wrath? (Ephesians, 4:26).

- What is the difference between anger and wrath?

2. Summarize what you have learned from this lesson by answering the questions below.

   - What strategy can you implement today to make a difference in your life?

3. What positive words have you spoken over your life that will bless you today and in the future?

4. What negative things (words) have you spoken over yourself that could become a curse in your life?

5. Can you identify the effects of previously spoken words (from childhood to now) that are still actively performing in your life?

   - What were the affirming words, wishes, or desires?

- What were the negative, self-defeating, and hurtful words spoken over your life?

6. What negative criticisms, destructive, or life-limiting sentences have you spoken over others that could be harming them today?

7. How can you reverse spoken words' adverse or destructive effects?

8. What measures do you employ to prevent or minimize contaminating forces from wreaking havoc in your life (people, food, clothing, buildings)?

Topic: Helpful Communication Patterns and Practices

Exercise: Think First

Instructions:

1. This is a two-person assignment (based upon comfort level).

2. Participate in Grand Rounds.

3. Participate in Group coaching.

4. Share what you have learned.

5. Continue journaling.

6. Listen to the Books of Proverbs, Psalm, or John.

Questions:

We have many questions that we ponder when going through challenging situations in life. Sometimes we have to search deep within our souls to find possible explanations and answers to what we do not understand to find meaning and reason. We cannot resist asking the following questions.

1. Are we digesting the meals we have served or treated ourselves or others?

2. How can we treat ourselves better?

3. How can we treat others better?

4. What negative thoughts, feelings, desires, criticism, and expectations have we released into the atmosphere about ourselves that has brought forth life and now haunts us?

5. Are you ready to reverse the effects by asking the Lord to forgive us of the errors in judgment? Are you willing to proceed with repenting and canceling the impact of negative thoughts, feelings, desires, criticism, etc.?

6. Like Job, sometimes the things we fear most become a reality in our lives. Fear comes from the enemy's kingdom because God does not give us the tormenting spirit of fear. Can we ask the Lord to strengthen our faith instead and remove the impact from our lives in fear?

7. What fears have we expressed that came upon us, and are we willing to repent for allowing the presence of fear to operate in our lives?

8. When we evaluate our problems, which biblical principles should we embrace to change our situation?

Topic: Know the Real Enemy

Exercise: The Counterfeit

Instructions:

1. Participate in Group coaching.

2. Share insights and revelations gained in this section.

3. Continue journaling.

4. Participate in Grand Rounds.

5. Make this a two-person assignment.

6. Listen to the Books of Proverbs, Psalm, or John.

Questions:

1. What are the commandments that Satan has adopted in his kingdom? (They oppose what God commands in Exodus chapter 20).

2. Below are statements that we have believed or adopted into our lives as truths. Identify the ones with which you agree.

    - You are the only God and ruler of your life.

    - You control your destiny in life.

- Your life is your own, and it's in your hands to commit suicide.

- Don't need anyone to tell me how to run my life.

- Life has no significant value.

- Human beings have become obsolete now that computers can do so much.

- There is no eternal salvation; there is no life beyond this earthly living.

- No need to believe in creation; it does not exist.

- You are only responsible to and for yourself.

- Reject everything that relates to God's commandments because they are offensive to you.

- Do it to them before they do it to you.

- No need to develop or exercise a conscience. Need to live free of conscience.

- Life is all about self, and thus, being selfish is ok.

- Self-fulfillment is the ultimate goal in life.

- Rejoice when you kill, steal, believe in lies, reject the truth, harm others, and live for obtaining money or possessions.

- There is no problem if you can cheat, betray, or manipulate others without feeling remorseful or shameful.

- It is ok not to forgive others because you have a right to be unforgiving and hold bitterness for the rest of your life.

- Allow your pain and disappointments to be the central core of your being.

- Share the horrible things in your life, so others know that you, too, have had challenging experiences worse than theirs.

- More power to you. All power belongs to you to do as you please.

- You should live in the past and make a home there. It's time to camp here forever.

- Demand from others and do not share or become a giver. Be a taker.

- Hoard information, talents, and treasures for yourself. It's your prerogative.

- I do not live for others. It's my life, and it's all about me, myself, and I.

- Having children is all centered around money issues. I can't afford to have children.

- Forget about the instructions to multiply and replenish the earth; that's for fools without ambition.

- The earth does not have the resources to feed or take care of more people.

- We should control the population through ethnic cleansing, abortions, incarceration, wars, genocides, etc. There are too many people on earth.

- Men rule the earth, and it belongs to the few wealthy ones.

- We, the selected few, know what's best for everyone else, and we make the decisions on this earth regarding the affairs of the rest of the world.

* Please note that all the above are lies from the enemy or inappropriate. Write your comments below.

3. How does an enemy bring growth, advancement, richness, betterment, and wisdom to your life?

4. Identify an incident or situation where you blamed someone for making you feel angry.

   - Did you ever feel victimized?

   - What were the issues surrounding this?

   - How did you feel, and how did others respond to you?

5. Meditate upon the following:

People influence us positively or negatively. But when we tend to blame others for our feelings of unhappiness, failures, discomfort, and lack of progress in life, we communicate to others about our inability to manage, control, and assume full responsibility for the interaction. People are never responsible for our responses, and we are the only ones who have total control over how we choose to react. Our reaction becomes the most critical issue in any conflict, and managing this is our responsibility. There is no need to blame others for how we feel or react. We must assume all responsibilities for our feelings as being generated by us and not others, even if they are the trigger. No one can make us feel a certain way because they are our responsibility and not theirs. What are your thoughts?

Topic: Who Is Your Enemy

Exercise: The Road to Recognition

Instructions:

1. Find a partner of your choosing to complete this exercise.

2. Share what you have learned with others.

3. Participate in Grand Rounds.

4. Participate in Group coaching.

5. Continue journaling.

6. Listen to the Books of Proverbs, Psalm, or John.

Questions:

1. What is the definition of an enemy?

2. What is the role of an enemy in your life?

3. Were you ever betrayed? What was your experience like, and how did it make you feel?

4. What personal characteristics or warning signals might you have overlooked during your relationship?

5. How would you deal with a friend who is indeed an enemy?

6. How have you hurt others while living in the kingdom of darkness?

7. How are you a friend to yourself?

8. How are you an enemy to yourself?

9. What can you do to become less of an enemy to yourself?

10. What are you willing to do in improving your relationships with those who have authority over you?

11. As a potential leader, what characteristics do you want from your followers?

Becoming A Great Leader at Home and in the Marketplace

- It is challenging to be a great leader unless you are a great follower.

- Building and maintaining relationships is the most critical responsibility of a leader.

- Followers need to know that you care about them as individuals and not just about job responsibilities.

- Understanding, mercy, equity, and fairness are important to followers.

- Practice love as your guiding post, along with clear expectations for improvement.

- Strive for excellence, not perfection.

- Recognize and deal with your enemies swiftly and concisely.

- If disrespected, respond swiftly and be clear about the consequences of repeat behavior. You shall never tolerate disrespect.

- Pattern your leadership from the life of Jesus Christ. He is the best teacher.

Topic: The Wounded Soul

Exercise: Access Granted

Instructions:

1. This is a two-person assignment.

2. Participate in Grand Rounds.

3. Participate in Group Coaching.

4. Share what you have learned with others.

5. Continue journaling.

6. Listen to the Books of Proverbs, Psalm, or John.

Questions and Assignment:

1. Take an inventory of family, friends, and associates. The center of the relationship circle is your heart. Number the circles from the center towards the edges. Place family and friends in the appropriate circles around your heart.

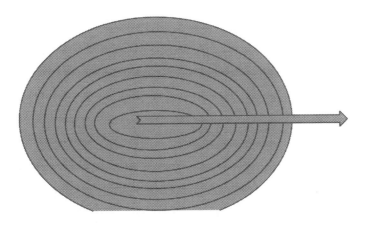

Developed and designed by Dr. Maxcelle Forrester

- Place the number 1 in the circle's center, which is your heart.

- Number the remaining circles from your heart outward to the end of the rings.

- Assign family members, co-workers, and friends to the appropriate circles from your heart.

- Explain why you placed each person in that circle away from your heart.

- What criteria did you use to determine who goes in which circle?

- What criteria would you use to promote individuals closer to your heart?

- What criteria would you use to demote individuals and move them farther from your heart?

- What determines how long a person should remain at the same level?

- What criteria do you use to expel someone from your network of circles?

- At what entry-level do you accept others into your life, and why?

- What determines when you close your circles to others?

- How many circles of friends do you need in your life?

- What purpose do circles of friends serve in your life?

- How do you maintain your circles of friends?

- How many enemies do you keep in your circles, and if so, what is the reason for keeping them?

2. Can you remember feeling like a victim?

  - What were the circumstances that made you feel like a victim?

  - What steps did you or could you have taken to change from a victim mentality to becoming a conqueror or a force to contend with courageously?

  - What advice would you give to someone with a victim mindset?

  - Who helped you become victorious, and what did you learn from the experiences?

- Have you ever experienced a sense of disappointment in yourself because you have failed? What happened?

- How did you overcome the feelings attached to failure?

- What lessons did you learn from having failed?

3. Below are warning signals (red flags) that produce stress, toxic emotions, and wounded relationships. When we see these behaviors in others, we must look within ourselves first to improve our lives. Sometimes, what we see reflects our mindsets, strengths, attitudes, or our weaknesses. We are all under construction and need help in self-improvement activities, but we must be aware of what's within and around us and their influences on our lives. We will become contaminated or do the same for others if not mindful of knowing when to separate ourselves. These are some signs and symptoms to guide us in evaluating ourselves and others.

   1. Hatred (towards self or others)

   2. Bitterness within their hearts, bitter root judgment

   3. Harboring Unforgiveness

   4. Violent and threatening

   5. Uncontrolled anger

   6. Injury to animals

   7. Injury to self

   8. Injury to others

9. Revengeful nature holds grudges and malice

10. Resentment

11. Severe mood swings

12. Double mindedness, won't make a decision or commit

13. Negativity, critical nature, cannot be pleased

14. Recurrent false accusations of others

15. Uncontrolled jealousy, stalking, no respect for personal rights or privacy

16. Rage, including road rage

17. The inclination or involvement in criminal activities, including misdemeanors

18. Retaliation, spiteful or getting even predisposition

19. Use of foul language

20. Constantly blames others, refuses to accept responsibility for actions

21. History of or is presently unfaithful, disloyal, or secretive

22. Ungrateful

23. Unthankful

24. Condescending attitude

25. Humiliates others privately or publicly

26. Controlling, no regards for feelings, input or choices and preferences of others

27. Defensive, rejects constructive criticism for improvement, unwilling to negotiate or adapt

28. Refuses to worship the living God of Abraham, Isaac, Jacob, and Israel

29. Selfish, wants all, inconsiderate, don't care attitude, hurtful

30. Greedy for gain, will steal, deceive, scam, or rob others

31. A taker and not a giver

32. Impulsive, inconsistent, or unpredictable

33. Lies cannot be believed or trusted, stories are inconsistent, dishonest

34. Proud, prideful, scornful

35. Risky behavior, careless, accident-prone, or Dare-devil behavior

36. Inconsiderate of others

37. Self-neglectful behavior, poor self-image, low self-esteem

38. Complainer, difficult to please, assumes no responsibility for own happiness

39. Lives beyond means, frequently broke, borrows and begs, slow or unwilling to repay

40. Poor money manager, no budget, spends on wants as a priority instead of means

41. Flirtatious behaviors, unsafe boundaries, irresponsible, attention seeker, distractor

42. Will not save for a rainy day

43. Unkind behavior, insensitive to the needs of others, gossips, meddles

44. Showoff, conceited, talks too much, nothing is sacred, makes self and others vulnerable

45. Plagued with conflicting relationships on different levels, including family

46. Dishonors parents, disrespectful and uncaring, and neglectful. Watch how a man treats his mother, expect equivalent treatment

47. Disrespects authority figures and dishonors leadership

48. Absent parenting, neglectful behavior, irresponsible attitudes towards their children

49. Stingy hands, miser, hoarder

50. Wasteful; waste leads to wants

51. Will not apologize, admit wrong, refuses to change despite the consequences, ignores partnership responsibilities

52. Lazy, refuses to work consistently

53. Childish behavior, temper tantrums, refusal to grow up, wants to be catered to at all times

54. No friends, unfriendly, prevents friendships from forming, does not entertain others

55. Too many friends, unable to establish priorities, unavailable

4. Select three character traits from the list above you need to improve upon or delete from your life. Do a word search in the Bible and select three verses to help you change and replace your thoughts, beliefs, and actions. Write them in your notebook and include the scripture verse.

The three habits or character traits I wish to change or delete are:

A.

B.

C.

7. Read and meditate on the following scriptures. What revelations did you find in these scriptures?

Proverbs 12:26

Proverbs 13:20

Proverbs 18:24

Proverbs 24:6

Proverbs 27:6

1st Corinthians 15:33

Proverbs 22:24-25

1st Corinthians 5:11

John 15:13

5. Select the habits and characters you desire to change from the list above and fill in the blank below. Read the prayer aloud as this is between you and God only. He wants to hear your voice.

Prayer

Father, I recognize that I have within me these habits & character flaws

_____

that do not allow me to maximize my potential in life. So, I repent for these habits and character flaws that have taken residence in my heart, soul, and mind. Please forgive and help me remove these from my life. I want blessings and prosperity as my inheritance that are already written about me in my book.

Help me walk in the paths of righteousness and live a life that reflects the kingdom of light. Spirit of God, I permit you to make the necessary changes so I can walk in the promises ordained for me before the foundations of the earth and before being conceived in my mother's womb. The plans you have for me are to bring prosperity, not harm, and give me hope and a future. You declare this to be so in Jeremiah 29:11 (NIV), and I want this glorious plan you have carved out just for me, with my name written on it.

I desire to adapt to Your will and Your ways. Forgive me for missing the mark and having the wrong motives and indiscretions. I repent for the iniquities of my ancestors back to the days of Adam. Please forgive them and cleanse me from all unrighteousness. I thank you in return with the expectation of a renewed heart and mind that reflects your glory.

I believe that Yeshua lived, died, and was resurrected from the dead to bring me salvation and abundant life here on earth and through eternity. I accept Him as Lord and Savior of my life. You have given us the name of Yeshua through whom we have access to your kingdom. Thank you for Your forgiveness, mercy, and grace that you extend to me through Yeshua. All that I am or ever hope to be; I give you, the God of Abraham, Isaac, Jacob, and Israel, the only true and living God. Thank you for your answered prayer. Amen.

Topic: Rescued From Dysfunction

Exercise: Wholeness

Instructions:

1. Read Genesis Chapters 1 & 2

2. Read aloud using the Bible (New King James Version is preferred but not required).

3. Read ten verses at a time and answer the questions below.

NOTATIONS:

1. Note that the Spirit of God is central to the creation and all its activities. God is a Spirit and has no flesh or body to cover Himself.

2. Note that the voice of God was instrumental in bringing things into being.

3. Note the orderly manner and the priorities established in creation.

4. Note that whatever He created was good, and he does not make junk or that which is useless.

5. Note the purposeful nature of how and when He produced items in the universe.

6. Note that He created man from nothing and formed and fashioned man into a living soul.

7. Note that He made us be like Him; in His image and Likeness.

8. Note that God puts His Spirit into man, and he starts to live.

9. Note that without the Spirit of God, man cannot live or stay alive.

10. Therefore, when God removes His Spirit, man is dead. His Spirit sustains our lives.

11. Note that the Garden of Eden, a Heavenly place, was made for man.

12. Note that earth is the only planet God deemed perfect for man's existence.

13. Note that man was required to work; therefore, work is healthy and beneficial. Work was God's plan from the beginning.

14. Note that man had directives or instructions to follow for his gain, and he did not decide what to do. The man worked with his hands, became productive, and fulfilled God's desire through work.

15. Note that man was created (out of nothing) and made (from the dust of the earth) in the image of God. But the woman came out of Adam's side, and she was crafted from his bone (rib).

16. Note that reproduction since creation comes out of man's loin.

17. Note that the woman and the man were equal partners, becoming one.

18. Note that the man and the woman were adults and not children at the creation time.

19. Note the only union that the Creator endorses is joining man and woman, and it is the only combination that leads to reproduction.

20. Note that God made a suitable companion and brought her to the man.

21. Note that woman was the crown creation; everything was there for her, including the man. God fashioned her specifically for him. He is a blessed man because a wife is a great blessing from God.

22. Note that together the man and the woman are humankind in God's vocabulary.

23. Note that God made opposite sexes to fulfill His purpose on the earth.

24. Note God is the Creator (Potter), and man is a created being (Clay).

25. Note that God directs, and a man follows; a parent-child relationship.

26. Note the importance of "seed" and its ability to multiply and replenish the earth.

27. Note that God finished everything He started, paying attention to details.

28. Note that God reviewed His work and approved it as good and very good.

29. Note that God developed the pattern and the blueprint for creation, including the universe.

30. Note that even God rested after working, and so should we. He designed 24 hours to rest after six days of working.

31. What else did you notice?

Questions:

1. What information leaped off the page in Genesis 1:1-10?

2. What adjectives would you use to describe the God of creation?

3. What thoughts do you believe existed in the mind of God when He created you?

4. What did you learn from these ten verses?

5. What surprised or fascinated you most about this section?

6. How do you see yourself, your role, responsibilities, and expectation as a created being?

7. What should your relationship be to the Creator?

8. What should your relationship be with the universe that hosts your habitation?

Topic: Foundation for A New Creation Part 1 & 2

Exercise: Hammer and nail

Instructions:

1. Read the scriptures in this section.

2. This is a two-person assignment.

3. Continue to update your journal.

4. Participate in Grand Rounds.

5. Participate in Group Coaching.

6. Share what you have learned.

Questions:

1. The Creator established only one way to redeem ourselves of wrongdoings and get back into His grace and kingdom. What is the process?

2. For what purpose was Jesus Christ born?

3. How should we handle moving forward and living without guilt, shame, condemnation, guilt, or regrets?

4. How do you benefit from the works Jesus did when He offered His life in exchange for the sins of all humanity?

5. "Greater love has no one than this, than to lay down one's life for his friends" (John 15:13).

   - How would you describe this expression of love?

   - How do you feel about someone loving you to that extent?

6. What benefits are you entitled to as a descendant of the Abrahamic Covenant? (Genesis 7:1-7).

Topic: Walk the Walk

Exercise: Entangled

Instructions:

1. This is a two-person assignment.

2. Participate in Grand Rounds.

3. Participate in Group Coaching.

4. Share what you have learned with others.

5. Continue journaling.

6. Listen to the Books of Psalm, Proverbs, or John.

Questions:

1. Which three scriptures have the most significant impact, and explain how they have influenced your understanding and application to your life?

2. Is your understanding of Yeshua (Jesus, Messiah) and God different from what you believed, and how are they different?

3. How could Yeshua assist you in understanding the root cause of problems, and how would this help solve them?

4. What are the Ten Commandments governing our lifestyle in Exodus 20? Which one do you need to practice more diligently and why?

5. Most people have felt emptiness, feeling lost, wanting, or incomplete within their souls.

   - What event or situation would precipitate these feelings?

   - How would one describe the feeling?

   - How do these influence communications with others during these times?

   - How is it possible to feel lonely in a crowded room?

   - What positive things can fill the emptiness inside?

   - What biblical principles or scripture verses would bring clarity and understanding in coping with life's adversities?

   - What instructions or advice would you give to others from this lesson on becoming an overcomer?

6. What kind of life would one expect to live in the kingdom of Life and Light in Jesus Christ?

7. What does it mean to be One with God?

Bibliography

Bevere, John. (2014). The Bait of Satan: Living Free from the Deadly Trap of Offense. Lake Mary: Charisma House.

Bishop, Markus. (1997). Our Covenant of Prosperity: Crossing the Threshold to Supernatural Abundance. Tulsa: Harrison House.

Bosworth, F.F. (2000). Christ Healer. New Kensington: Whitaker House.

Bynum, Juanita. (2002). My Spiritual Inheritance: Walking In Your Destiny. Lake Mary: Charisma House.

Capps, Charles. (1987). God's Creative Power for Healing. England: Capps Publishing.

Cerullo, Morris. (2012). Demolishing Demonic Strongholds: Spiritual Firepower. Shippensburg: Destiny Image Publishers, Inc.

Copeland, Kenneth. & Gloria. (1999). One Word from God Can Change Your Health. Tulsa: Harrison House, Inc.

Copeland, Kenneth. (1974). The Laws of Prosperity. Tulsa: Harrison House, Inc.

Copeland, Kenneth. The Force of Righteousness (10th Printing). Tulsa: Harrison House.

Covey, Stephen. R. (1990). The 7 Habits of Highly Effective People: Powerful Lessons in Personal Change. New York: Simon & Schuster.

Covey, Stephen. R. (1995). First Things First. New York: Simon & Schuster.

Damazio, Frank. (1988). The Making of a Leader: Biblical Leadership Principles for Today's Leaders. Portland: City Christian Publishing. Dollar (Jr), Creflo. (1993). The Divine Order of Faith. Edmond: Vision Communications.

Holy Bible: New International Version. (1983). Grand Rapids: Zondervan Publishing House.

Levy, Mary Ann. (2017). The Luciferian Strategy. Nigeria: Spiritual Life Outreach Inc.

MacArthur, John. (2001). The Keys to Spiritual Growth: Unlocking the Riches of God. Wheaton: Crossway Books.

Madugba, Chinyere. G. (2002). Brokenness: An Inevitable Experience for Spiritual Significance. Nigeria: Spiritual Life Outreach Inc.

Madugba, Chinyere. (2013). Impacting Your World. Nigeria: Spiritual Life Outreach Inc.

Madugba, Mosy. (2003). Dealing With Evil Foundations at Various Levels. Nigeria: Spiritual Life Outreach Inc.

Maxwell, John. C. (2015). Intentional Living: Choosing a Life That Matters. New York: Hachette Book Group.

Messer, Ralph. Rabbi. (2014). The Genesis Factor Year 1: Kingdom Principles For Kingdom Living. Parker: Simchat Torah Beit Midrash Publishing.

Meyer, Joyce. (1987). Beauty for Ashes: Receiving Emotional Healing. Tulsa: Harrison House.

Meyer, Joyce. (1995). Battlefield Of The Mind: Winning the Battle in Your Mind. New York: Hachette Book Groups, Inc.

Murdock, Mike. (1999). The Law of Recognition: Discovering the Gifts, Opportunities & Relationships That God Has Already Placed in Your Life. Denton: Wisdom International.

The Nelson Study Bible: New King James Version. (1982). Nashville: Thomas Nelson Publishers.

Parsley, Rod. (1995). Ten Golden Keys to Your Abundance. Columbus: Results Publishing.

Sande, Ken. (2004). The Peace Maker: A Biblical Guide to Resolving Personal Conflict. Grand Rapids: Baker Books.

Thomas, Rick. (2003). Capturing the mind of God: A Life-Changing Vision of Your Future. Charlotte: LifeBridge Books.

Thomas, Rick. (2005). Significant Seed: Perpetual Harvest. Charlotte: LifeBridge Books.

Vanzant, Iyanla. (1998). Yesterday I Cried: Celebrating the Lessons of Living And Loving. New York: Simon & Schuster.

Printed in the United States
by Baker & Taylor Publisher Services